Our Hope in Christ

A Chapter Analysis Study of 1 Thessalonians

DESIGN FOR DISCIPLESHIP

DFD7

NAVPRESS®

BRINGING TRUTH TO LIFE

OUR GUARANTEE TO YOU

We believe so strongly in the message of our books that we are making this quality guarantee to you. If for any reason you are disappointed with the content of this book, return the title page to us with your name and address and we will refund to you the list price of the book. To help us serve you better, please briefly describe why you were disappointed. Mail your refund request to: NavPress, P.O. Box 35002, Colorado Springs, CO 80935.

The Navigators is an international Christian organization. Our mission is to advance the gospel of Jesus and His kingdom into the nations through spiritual generations of laborers living and discipling among the lost. We see a vital movement of the gospel, fueled by prevailing prayer, flowing freely through relational networks and out into the nations where workers for the kingdom are next door to everywhere.

NavPress is the publishing ministry of The Navigators. The mission of NavPress is to reach, disciple, and equip people to know Christ and make Him known by publishing life-related materials that are biblically rooted and culturally relevant. Our vision is to stimulate spiritual transformation through every product we publish.

ISBN 1-60006-010-2

Cover design by Arvid Wallen
Cover illustration by Michael Halbert
Interior design by The DesignWorks Group
Creative Team: Dan Rich, Kathy Mosier, Arvid Wallen, Pamela Poll, Pat Reinheimer

Original DFD Author: Chuck Broughton
Revision Team: Dennis Stokes, Judy Gomoll, Christine Weddle, Ralph Ennis

Printed in the United States of America

1 2 3 4 5 6 / 10 09 08 07 06

FOR A FREE CATALOG OF NAVPRESS BOOKS & BIBLE STUDIES,
CALL 1-800-366-7788 (USA) OR 1-800-839-4769 (CANADA)

DFD7 | CONTENTS

LIFETIME ADVENTURE

> For everything that was written in the past was written to teach us, so that through endurance and the encouragement of the Scriptures we might have hope.
>
> ROMANS 15:4

In giving us His written word, the Bible, God longs to encourage us. He invites us into the exhilarating adventure of personal Bible study to fill us with hope. As the Lord fills our minds with His truth, He also ushers us into more intimate fellowship with Him — fellowship that satisfies our hearts and changes our lives.

In *Our Hope in Christ*, Book Seven of *Design for Discipleship*, you will learn how to study New Testament books chapter by chapter. You will gain an understanding of Bible study principles and methods. Each chapter will highlight a different study skill or resource that will equip you to continue to explore the Bible for yourself as a lifetime habit.

The method you'll use in studying 1 Thessalonians can be termed "book analysis." It is a different type of Bible study that will involve your own firsthand research. Your study will include three basic steps.

First is a **Survey** of the entire book. Rather than concentrate on particular details, you will work to gain a broad overview of the whole.

Next you will do a **Chapter-by-Chapter Analysis** of 1 Thessalonians. Your aim here is to study the five chapters separately, focusing on the specific truths and insights which you will discover in each chapter.

Third is a **Summary** of 1 Thessalonians. After studying the five chapters in detail, you will now pull together what you have learned and write down your conclusions. In developing your summary, many of you will express yourself through writing, but some of you may find it easier to express yourself in a different manner (drawing, poetry). Please feel free to develop a creative summary in a manner that clearly communicates what you are learning.

Ask for the Holy Spirit's guidance as you work on each step. Psalm 119:34 is a good prayer: "Give me understanding, and I will keep your law and obey it with all my heart."

You will probably find it best not to refer to Bible commentaries until after you have completed your study of each chapter. Allow the Holy Spirit to speak to you directly from the Scriptures.

Book Analysis

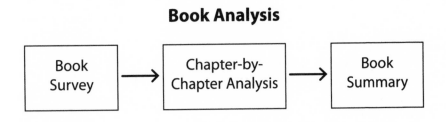

1

1 Thessalonians: Your Survey

The purpose of surveying a book you want to study is to gain a broad overview of its setting and themes. As you survey 1 Thessalonians, you will be laying a valuable foundation for the discoveries you make later when you study each chapter in detail. Do your best now to gain a good understanding of the background and general themes of this book.

The most important thing you can do to become familiar with 1 Thessalonians is simply to read it over and over again thoughtfully. In most Bibles, Paul's first letter to the Thessalonians is only three to five pages long. So it will only take a few minutes to read through the book without stopping. This is a good time to read the book from different Bible translations and paraphrases. Also try reading the book aloud at least once. Many people enjoy listening to the book on tape as well, because sometimes we notice things when we hear them that we missed while reading silently.

Keep track here of how many times you read through 1 Thessalonians: _____

Reading becomes studying when you add pen and paper and begin to take notes on what you are learning. It may be helpful for you to photocopy 1 Thessalonians from your preferred translation so that you can mark it up freely as you study. Your written book survey will contain six main sections: principal personalities, historical setting, purpose, themes, questions, and an overview.

Book Survey

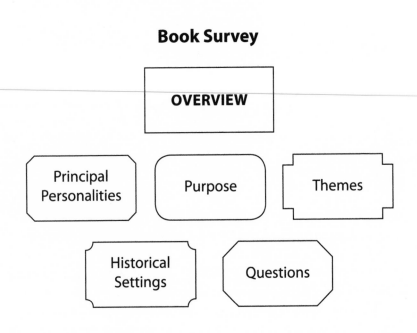

PRINCIPAL PERSONALITIES

1. Which of his fellow workers did Paul list as coauthors of this letter? (1 Thessalonians 1:1)

2. How did Paul describe the Thessalonian believers in the opening sentence of the letter?

Thessalonica — the modern-day city of Salonika in Greece — is first mentioned in the Bible in Acts 17:1-13. Read this passage to answer questions 3-5.

3. When Paul arrived in Thessalonica, where did he begin to preach?

4. What message did Paul give to the Thessalonians?

5. Describe the various responses in Thessalonica to Paul's teaching.

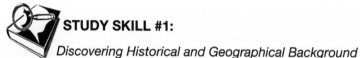

STUDY SKILL #1:

Discovering Historical and Geographical Background

Try to get a sense of where these historical events occurred by locating and writing the names of key cities, regions/provinces, and other geographical places on the map on the next page. Rather than provide a completed map, we invite you to do your own research. Consult a Bible atlas, maps at the back of a study Bible, or online resources such as www.gospelcom.net, www.biblegateway.com, or www.crosswalk.com to locate the places listed below.

REGIONS: Thracia, Macedonia, Achaia, Asia, Galatia

CITIES: Thessalonica, Philippi, Amphipolis, Appolia, Berea, Philippi, Athens, Corinth, Ephesus

OTHER: Aegean Sea, Crete

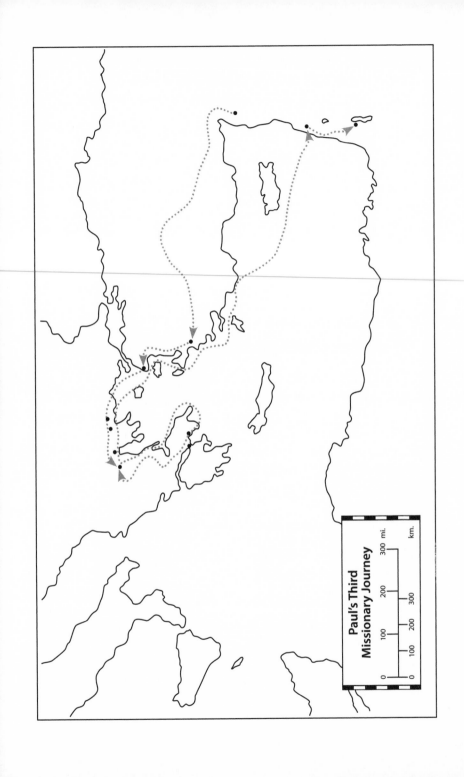

Paul's Third
Missionary Journey

300 mi.

km.

0   100   200   300

0   100   200   300

6. Record here what else you learn from reference books (such as Bible dictionaries, study Bibles, and encyclopedias) about the historical background of Thessalonica, the church there, and this letter.

PURPOSE

7. From your own reading of 1 Thessalonians and from reference books, what reasons can you give for Paul writing this letter? Consider questions he tried to answer, circumstances that the Thessalonians were facing, needs he responded to, and possible problems he addressed to help you determine his purpose.

8. What major themes of this letter stand out to you?

9. What are some of the secondary themes you find?

10. List key words that occur frequently and other important words in 1 Thessalonians. Consider marking each key word with a different color marker to help you trace themes visually through the book.

> **"** People whose lives are oriented around Christ don't just study the Bible to be smarter. They see that every single page of [his Word] is stained with the crimson blood of Jesus himself. Suddenly, the Bible isn't just a text to be studied but a source of life for a withering branch.
>
> —Eric Sandras, PhD, *Buck-Naked Faith*

QUESTIONS

11. What questions have surfaced as you surveyed 1 Thessalonians? These might reflect topics that arouse your curiosity, topics you want to learn more about, terms or facts to clarify, or things that confuse you. Write them here as you read and study.

In the overview section of your book survey, your aim is to summarize the book concisely by writing a brief outline. As a starting point you may want to refer to the paragraph/section headings included in most translations or to outlines given in study Bibles. But remember that chapter divisions and verse numbers and subtopics were not included in the original documents; they were added later to help locate particular passages. So feel free to organize your outline in any way that makes sense to you.

For example, the last four verses in chapter 2 express Paul's longing to see the Thessalonians, the same theme he continues into chapter 3. So you may want to study 1 Thessalonians 2:17–3:13 as one unit.

Under each heading you choose, use either short phrases or summary sentences to describe the various parts of the book. Try to keep your outline brief for now.

It may seem difficult at this point to prepare an adequate outline. But the exercise will help you gain an overall view of the book when you later study each chapter more thoroughly. At the close of your study of 1 Thessalonians you will have the opportunity to review the whole book again, and to revise your outline if necessary.

12. Use the following space to write your survey outline of 1 Thessalonians.

Close your overview by writing a brief title for the whole book of 1 Thessalonians that captures its central heart and message for you. Also select one or two verses that you consider key to the whole book. Spend some time meditating, memorizing, and praying over your key verse.

13. BOOK TITLE:

14. KEY VERSE(S):

Remember that the study of God's living Word is a journey into the heart and mind of God. As you reflect on 1 Thessalonians, what are some key ideas revealed about the heart and mind of God?

While you may choose to write out these key ideas, some of you may also prefer to identify ideas in a more creative manner (drawing, poetry). Please feel free to express yourself in a way that is natural to you.

2

1 Thessalonians: Chapter 1

Have you ever imagined the Bible as a whole library—a library stocked with sixty-six books written by many people but ultimately authored by God Himself? Picture yourself pulling the book of 1 Thessalonians off the "shelf" and devoting the next several weeks to soaking yourself in the truths and riches contained in this one book. Then imagine yourself spending the rest of your life enjoying one book after another, and becoming a man or woman of the Word! That is the promise of a lifetime of Bible study. The skills you develop now and the resources you learn to use will equip you for a lifetime of personal exploration of the Word of God.

After completing your survey, you are ready to study the first chapter of 1 Thessalonians. When working on your written analysis of each chapter, you will begin with a *passage description*, then do a *verse-by-verse meditation*, and finish with your *conclusions*. These will help you in making a personal *application* from your study, which you will also record in writing.

Chapter Analysis

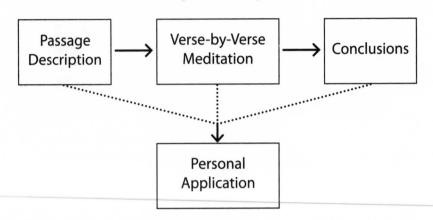

As you study this chapter, keep track of how many times you have read it: _____

STUDY SKILL #2:

Comparing Different Bible Translations and Paraphrases

Before beginning your written work, read through the first chapter several times, perhaps jotting down a few notes on things that stand out to you.

You may want to supplement your reading with a modern paraphrase, such as *The Message* (MSG), the *New Living Translation* (NLT), the *Phillips* translation (PH), or others. The *Amplified Bible* (AMP) is helpful for exploring the shades of meaning for key words in the original text. However, for your focused chapter analysis study be sure to choose a basic translation such as the *New International Version* (NIV) or the *New King James Version* (NKJV).

PASSAGE DESCRIPTION

After reading through the chapter, your first step in analyzing it is to briefly describe the overall content. At this point do not attempt to interpret what you read. Your aim is to carefully observe and summarize **what** is said, not **why**.

One method of describing a passage is to rewrite it — omitting any modifying words and phrases that are not grammatically necessary — so that you express the central meaning of the sentence. This basically leaves the nouns and verbs. It is especially effective when the passage contains many descriptive words.

For example, here are verses 2 and 3 of the first chapter written in this manner:

2 — We thank God for you.

3 — We remember before God your work, your labor,
and your endurance.

With this method you can quickly observe the movement of the passage.

Another method of describing the chapter is to make an outline. The first step is to divide the passage into paragraphs. (Most recent Bible translations already have suggested paragraph breaks. The original text was not divided into paragraphs, so you may decide to divide the passage differently if that makes more sense to you.) After determining your paragraph divisions, write a sentence or two summarizing each paragraph's contents. Don't worry about omitting some details, but give a general framework which you can fit the details into later.

Here is a sentence summary of verses 2 and 3 as they might appear in a summary outline of the first chapter:

Paul tells how thankful he is for the quality
of life in the Thessalonian church (verses 2-3).

Use the space below to write a passage description of verses 4-10, either rewriting it without modifiers, or making a summary outline.

VERSE-BY-VERSE MEDITATION

The heart of your study of 1 Thessalonians occurs as you meditate on each verse of each chapter. Here you will pause to process and understand each verse before moving to the next. Do this prayerfully (not just academically) by asking the Holy Spirit to help you unpack and understand the message of each verse.

You will record your thoughts in this section under four headings: Observations, Questions and Answers, Cross-References, and Notes and Comments.

Under Observations, you will simply give attention to what the passage actually says. Here are some questions that can help you make accurate observations:

- *Who are the people involved?*
- *What ideas or teachings are expressed?*
- *What events happen?*
- *What are the stated results of these ideas or events?*
- *Where does this take place?*
- *What reasons or purposes are stated?*
- *How are things accomplished?*

Here are *observations* based on verses 2 and 3:

2 — Paul gave thanks for the Thessalonians.
3 — Three parallel thoughts in his prayers:
    a. work of faith
    b. labor of love
    c. endurance of hope

Because it is impractical to record every observation you make on a verse, record the observations that stimulate you to further thinking. But don't overlook the obvious!

Recording **Questions and Answers** takes considerable time and effort, but it often leads to rewarding meditation. As you grow in your knowledge of the Bible, the more questions you will have, and the more penetrating and significant they will be. At the same time, your knowledge and understanding will increase.

Here are possible questions for verses 2 and 3:

2 — What did Paul pray for them?

3 — What is faith? Answer: Trusting in God's character and obeying Him.

Why is endurance inspired by hope?

When a question has several possible answers, record as many answers as you can. The Scriptures do not always provide clear-cut answers on every issue, so be careful not to insist on always finding one. Major on what God has plainly revealed. Often it is best to write questions without writing an answer. This allows you more time to think about them. Later you can record the answers as you discover them.

In the third column of your chapter analysis, record **Cross-References** for some of the verses you are studying. In many cases a question you write will stimulate further study in other parts of the Bible that relate closely to the verse you are studying. The Bible is its own best commentary. Scripture interprets Scripture. The content of one passage clarifies the content of another.

Here are some cross-references for verses 2 and 3:

Verse 2 — 1 Thessalonians 5:18 — Giving thanks in everything.

Verse 3 — 2 Thessalonians 3:5 — Christ's perseverance.

Verse 3 — Hebrews 11:1 — Faith is confident assurance of the unseen and the future.

Good sources of cross-references are your own previous Bible study and verses you may have already memorized. If you cannot find a cross-reference on your own, use a concordance or the marginal notes in your Bible (more on these resources in later chapters).

Use the space in the *Notes and Comments* column to record additional personal insights and especially ideas God may be impressing on your heart for possible application. Also record information about people or places mentioned, as well as definitions of key words.

Use the charts on the following pages to record your thoughts as you meditate verse by verse through the first chapter of 1 Thessalonians.

Observations	Questions and Answers

Cross-References	Notes and Comments

CONCLUSIONS

By now you have done quite a bit of study. You have described the chapter, meditated on each verse, made observations, asked questions, discovered some answers, and found cross-references, as well as having made other notes and comments. Now you can begin to bring all this together by drawing some conclusions.

The **theme** is the central issue discussed by Paul in this chapter. Look back over your written work and ask, "What is the basic subject of this chapter? What is Paul talking about?" Record your answer here:

Along with finding a theme, you will also want to record **other conclusions** you make. Here is one example of a possible conclusion from this chapter:

Praying, preaching, and demonstrating God's power are keys to communicating the Gospel (verses 2,5).

Use the following space to record other conclusions you have from 1 Thessalonians 1.

You will also want to **title** the chapter. Your title will probably reflect the theme and conclusions you listed earlier. Record your title here:

Also **select one verse** that either captures the central truth of this chapter, or select any verse that touches your heart for personal reasons. Write it here, and consider memorizing it so that you can meditate on it over the next days and weeks. Record your key or favorite verse here:

APPLICATION

Writing out your application will help you clarify what you plan to do. It also encourages you to be specific. The following questions can help you apply the Bible to your life.

1. What does this passage have to say about God's view of reality?
2. How does this passage impact my intimacy with Him?
3. How does this passage speak to the issues and attitudes of my heart?
4. How does this passage impact my relationships with other people and with the natural world?
5. What specific step of action does God want me to take in response to this passage?

In the following space record your planned application from 1 Thessalonians 1.

As you continue your journey into the heart and mind of God, journal some key ideas revealed to you.

3

1 Thessalonians: Chapter 2

An open mind is necessary for effective Bible study. And you must also have a willingness to change your life. Whenever you hold back an area of your life from God's purposes, you will be hindered in understanding the Scriptures. So approach your Bible study with an open mind and a willing spirit. As you meditate on the second chapter, ask yourself why the Holy Spirit included this portion in Scripture.

Begin by reading 1 Thessalonians chapter 2 several times, perhaps in different translations. Briefly describe the overall content of 1 Thessalonians 2. Either rewrite it without including descriptive words and phrases, or make a summary outline. Or you may want to paraphrase the entire chapter.

Keep track here of the number of times you read through 1 Thessalonians chapter 2: _____

STUDY SKILL #3:

Finding Cross-References

The third column in your chapter analysis is devoted to cross-references. A cross-reference is a verse or passage found elsewhere in the book or the Bible that expresses a similar thought to the verse you are studying. In many cases a question you write will stimulate further study in other parts of the Bible that relate closely to the verse you are studying. The Bible is its own best commentary. Scripture interprets Scripture. The content of one passage clarifies the content of another.

Possible cross-references for this chapter include Acts 16:23-24 for the second verse, Galatians 1:10 for the fourth verse, 1 Corinthians 4:14-15 for verse 11, and Colossians 1:10 for verse 12.

Good sources of cross-references are your own previous Bible study and verses you may have already memorized. If you cannot find a cross-reference on your own, use a concordance or the marginal notes in your Bible. For this chapter try using several of these methods for finding cross-references. Record them in the chart on the next page.

Cross-References	Notes and Comments

Paul also wrote another letter to the Thessalonians approximately six months after writing his first letter. Consider reading 2 Thessalonians to discover what else he had to say to the young believers in Thessalonica about these same topics. What new light does 2 Thessalonians shed on your understanding of 1 Thessalonians? Summarize a few insights here.

Observations	Questions and Answers

CONCLUSIONS

What do you consider to be the major theme of 1 Thessalonians 2?

What other conclusions do you have from your study of this chapter?

What title would you give this chapter?

What is the key or favorite verse from this chapter?

APPLICATION

Application begins with our willingness to accept the truth God reveals. A sincere response to God's living Word is characterized by trust, obedience, praise, and thanksgiving. Your application may include:

- *remembering an impressive truth,*
- *changing a wrong attitude, or*
- *taking a positive action.*

Record your application plan here:

As you continue your journey into the heart and mind of God, journal some key ideas revealed to you.

4

1 Thessalonians: Chapter 3

Because of his love for the Thessalonian believers, Paul took specific action to encourage them, which is described in the third chapter of 1 Thessalonians. Review your written work on the first two chapters as you begin to study Paul's description of this action.

In addition to your own choice of cross-references, consider these possible cross-references for 1 Thessalonians 3:

Verse 4	Philippians 1:29
Verse 5	1 Peter 5:8
Verse 8	3 John 4
Verse 10	Colossians 4:12
Verse 12	1 Thessalonians 4:9-10
Verse 13	1 John 3:2-3

Observations	Questions and Answers

Cross-References	Notes and Comments

CONCLUSIONS

THEME:

OTHER CONCLUSIONS:

TITLE:

KEY OR FAVORITE VERSE:

APPLICATION

Review your application from the last chapter. Record how you are doing with it, along with any further thoughts.

Record the number of times you read this chapter in your study preparations: _____

STUDY SKILL #4:

Personal Application

It has been said that meditation without application leads to frustration! Studying the Bible without responding to what it says and applying it in your life only leads to intellectual knowledge. Application involves allowing the Scripture to influence your heart and putting its truths and principles into practice in your life. God wants you to recognize His personal message *to you* from this portion of Scripture, and respond accordingly. The psalmist wrote, "I have considered my ways and have turned my steps to your statutes. I will hasten and not delay to obey your commands" (Psalm 119:59-60).

The true benefit of Bible study is in knowing God deeply, receiving His instruction, and putting it into practice through your obedience. Application doesn't happen automatically simply by completing your study; it involves your personal decision and action.

Perhaps the Lord already has impressed you through some portion of the chapter about an application you should make. If not, prayerfully go back over the chapter and your study to find what He wants you to put into practice in your life. Again consider these five questions as you seek to apply God's Word.

1. What does this passage have to say about God's view of reality?
2. How does this passage impact my intimacy with Him?
3. How does this passage speak to the issues and attitudes of my heart?
4. How does this passage impact my relationships with other people and with the natural world?
5. What specific step of action does God want me to take in response to this passage?

Record your application here:

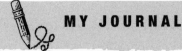

As you continue your journey into the heart and mind of God, journal some key ideas revealed to you.

CHAPTER

5

1 Thessalonians:
Chapter 4

STUDY SKILL #5:

Key Words and Phrases

By now you are noticing certain key words and phrases that Paul uses several times in his letter to the Thessalonians. Make a list of these key words and phrases below. Consider going through each chapter and marking each key word with a different color marker to help you trace themes visually through the book. For example, find each reference to "the return of Christ" in green, and each reference to "joy" in blue.

Key Words and Phrases from 1 Thessalonians:

Observations	Questions and Answers

Cross-References	Notes and Comments

CONCLUSIONS

THEME:

OTHER CONCLUSIONS:

TITLE:

KEY OR FAVORITE VERSE:

Review your application from the last chapter. Record any further thoughts or progress.

These questions can help you write meaningful applications:

1. What is the truth I want to apply?
2. What is my need?
3. What is my plan of action?
4. How will I assess my progress?

Pray for the Holy Spirit's help in selecting and carrying out your application.

Record here the number of times you read this chapter in your study preparation: _____

As you continue your journey into the heart and mind of God, journal some key ideas revealed to you.

6

1 Thessalonians: Chapter 5

STUDY SKILL #6:

Using Bible Resources

There are many Bible resources available to help in your study of Scripture. Consider obtaining some of these over time as valuable aids to your growth and spiritual transformation.

1. **Study Bibles** — usually contain extensive footnotes explaining individual verses, maps and charts, summaries of books and characters, archaeological information, as well as introductions and overviews of each book of the Bible.

2. **Bible Atlas** — provides extensive maps reflecting geographical information from various time periods in the Bible, traces the paths taken by biblical people in their travels, and so on.

3. **Bible Dictionaries** — list key important words from the Bible along with their definitions, etymologies (explaining the language source of each word), and background about each term. They may also contain cultural and historical information.

4. **Concordance** — lists many words used in the Bible along with detailed references where each word is used in the Bible. They may be published separately or included at the back of a study Bible. When you can't remember where a particular verse is located, a concordance can help you find it.

5. **Commentary** — a book or set of books written by various Bible scholars containing that person's interpretation of Bible passages. If you are having trouble understanding a verse or passage, you can consult a reliable commentary (or more than one).

6. **Online Resources** — Most of these resources described can also be found online at sites such as www.gospelcom.net, www.biblegateway.com, or www.crosswalk.com. Consider exploring these sites (or others like them) to see what is available. Be careful that the sites you visit are reputable and trustworthy, since there are many questionable sites on the Internet.

Observations	Questions and Answers

Cross-References	Notes and Comments

CONCLUSIONS

THEME:

OTHER CONCLUSIONS:

TITLE:

KEY OR FAVORITE VERSE:

1. Is there a *sin* for me to avoid?
2. Is there a *promise* from God for me to claim?
3. Is there an *example* for me to follow?
4. Is there a *command* for me to obey?
5. How can this passage increase my *knowledge* about God or about Jesus Christ?

You can remember these five questions by the word SPECK — sin, promise, example, command, and knowledge.

Pray for the Holy Spirit's help in selecting and carrying out your application.

Record here the number of times you read this chapter in your study preparation: _____

As you continue your journey into the heart and mind of God, journal some key ideas revealed to you.

1 Thessalonians: Your Summary

N ow you are ready to do a summary of 1 Thessalonians to get a unified picture of the book. First, try to think through 1 Thessalonians chapter by chapter without referring to the book or to your written work. On the following pages, write from memory a brief description of the contents of each chapter.

CHAPTER 1

CHAPTER 2

CHAPTER 3

CHAPTER 4

CHAPTER 5

Your next step is to **reread the book several times**. Do each reading at one sitting if possible. Because the material is now familiar, you should be able to read it rapidly. Look again for the general thread that runs through the book. Try to get an overall view.

Record here how many times you reread 1 Thessalonians for your summary study: _____

Next, review the **THEMES** you listed for each chapter. Choose those which seem most important to you now and list them here:

Also review your **CONCLUSIONS** for each chapter, choose the main ones and list them below. List also any conclusions you have on the book as a whole now that you have studied each chapter.

Review the **TITLES** you gave each chapter. Rewrite them here, making any changes you desire:

CHAPTER 1

CHAPTER 2

CHAPTER 3

CHAPTER 4

CHAPTER 5

Now consider the book as a whole and give it a **TITLE**. Try to keep your title short and use words that illustrate well the content of 1 Thessalonians. Record your title here:

As part of drawing conclusions about 1 Thessalonians, respond to these evaluative questions:

1. I would turn to 1 Thessalonians first if a question came up about . . .

2. If this book had not been included in the Bible, what would we miss most?

3. What does 1 Thessalonians communicate about the heart of God?

Other questions?

Finally, look back over the **APPLICATION PLANS** you recorded. Are there any you have not completed which you would now be able to carry out? Now write an application summary.

Consider these five questions as you seek to apply God's Word from 1 Thessalonians.

1. What does this passage have to say about God's view of reality?
2. How does this passage impact my intimacy with Him?
3. How does this passage speak to the issues and attitudes of my heart?
4. How does this passage impact my relationships with other people and with the natural world?
5. What specific step of action does God want me to take in response to this passage?

Pray for the Holy Spirit's help in selecting and carrying out your application.

 **STUDY SKILL #7:**

Making a Mind Map

Create a mind map for the book you have studied. It might reflect key things you learned from your study. Or it may reflect remaining questions and things you are genuinely curious about, which may lead to further study.

What is a mind map? Mind maps were promoted in the late 1960s by Tony Buzan and others (in books such as *The Mind Map Book,* Penguin, 1991). Think of a mind map as productive doodling! As a learning and thinking tool, a mind map is a great way to express your brainstorming thoughts using just key words and images. Here is how to make a mind map:

1. With your paper in landscape format, write the CENTRAL IDEA in a circle in the center.

2. Branching off from the central circle, look for ideas that connect or relate to the CENTRAL IDEA. Write in capital letters several broad SUBTOPICS related to the central idea. Use different colors, symbols, arrows, or shapes to express how these SUBTOPICS are connected to the CENTRAL IDEA.

3. Radiating from each of the SUBTOPICS write any EXAMPLES or DETAILS that you associate with that SUBTOPIC.

4. This is a creative brainstorming and summary tool, so don't analyze too much. Just draw quickly.

5. Keep adding ideas until you can't think of anything else to add, as depicted in the illustration.

The purpose of a mind map is to help you process a topic, question, or problem and explore its various aspects visually.

Mind Map

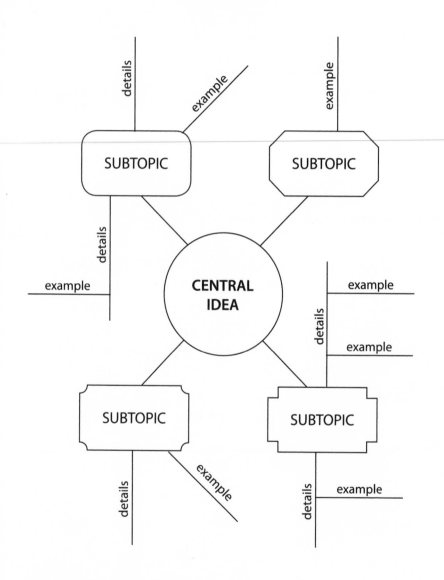

Here is just one way to visualize 1 Thessalonians:

Mind Map Example

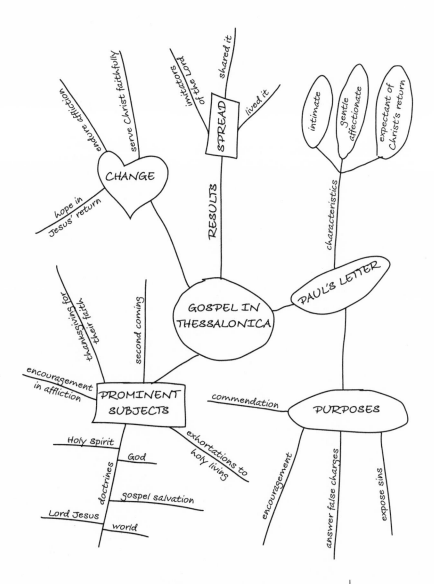

Close your study of Paul's letter to his friends in Thessalonica by drawing your own mind map reflecting what you remember and what touched you most from this book of the Bible. Create your own SUBTOPICS, as well as related ideas and connected words. Enjoy!

Congratulations! You've just completed a thorough study of one book of the Bible. Just sixty-five more to go, but don't be overwhelmed. Rather look forward to a lifelong journey into the heart and mind of God. We encourage you to continue studying the Scriptures with a group. Learn from each other. Grow together. And reach out to others — your family and networks of friends. Some may wish to study the Bible with you. Others will observe your life as you continue to get to know God and apply His living Word.

THE ESSENTIAL BIBLE STUDY SERIES FOR TWENTY-FIRST-CENTURY FOLLOWERS OF CHRIST.

DFD 1
Your Life in Christ   1-60006-004-8

This concise, easy-to-follow Bible study reveals what it means to accept God's love for you, keep Christ at the center of your life, and live in the power of the Spirit.

DFD 2
The Spirit-Filled Follower of Jesus   1-60006-005-6

Learn what it means to be filled by the Spirit so that obedience, Bible study, prayer, fellowship, and witnessing become natural, meaningful aspects of your life.

DFD 3
Walking with Christ   1-60006-006-4

Learn five vital aspects to living as a strong and mature disciple of Christ through this easy-to-understand Bible study.

DFD 4
The Character of a Follower of Jesus   1-60006-007-2

This insightful, easy-to-grasp Bible study helps you understand and put into action the internal qualities and values that should drive your life as a disciple of Christ.

DFD 5
Foundations for Faith   1-60006-008-0

This compelling Bible study will help you get a disciple's perspective on God, His Word, the Holy Spirit, spiritual warfare, and Christ's return.

DFD 6
Growing in Discipleship   1-60006-009-9

This study will provide insight and encouragement to help you grow as a true disciple of Christ by learning to share the blessings you've received from God.

DFD Leader's Guide
                                                   1-60006-011-0

The leader's guide provides all the insight and information needed to share the essential truths of discipleship with others, whether one-on-one or in small groups.

Visit your local Christian bookstore, call NavPress at 1-800-366-7788, or log on to www.navpress.com to purchase.
To locate a Christian bookstore near you, call 1-800-991-7747.

NAVPRESS
BRINGING TRUTH TO LIFE
www.navpress.com